HONG KONG TRAVEL GUIDE 2023:

Explore and Maximize the Hidden Gems in Hong Kong

BY

ALBERTA NELSON

Table Of Contents

Conclusion

Introduction

Hi there, I'm glad you made it here, in this Introductory section- I'll be sharing with you my personal experiences - my story

Come with me, let go......

There was a young woman named Alberta who had always dreamt of visiting the vibrant city of Hong Kong. The bustling streets, the stunning skyline, and the rich cultural heritage fascinated her. However, life seemed to have other plans for Alberta, as she faced numerous obstacles on her journey to this enchanting destination.

Alberta's difficulties began with the sheer logistics of planning the trip. She had to juggle her work commitments, personal responsibilities, and financial limitations. With each passing day, her dream seemed to drift further away, and she couldn't help but feel disheartened.

Feeling overwhelmed, Alberta confided in her close friend, Emily. Sensing Alberta's despair, Emily decided to lend a helping hand. She researched extensively, gathering information about flights, accommodations, and local attractions. Emily's dedication and thoroughness surprised Alberta, who felt a glimmer of hope rekindling within her.

One day, Emily handed Alberta a guidebook filled with colorful pages and detailed descriptions of Hong Kong's hidden gems. "This guidebook will be your companion throughout your journey," Emily said, a warm smile on her face. "It contains everything you need to know about Hong Kong, from the must-visit landmarks to the best local eateries."

Alberta held the guidebook in her hands, grateful for her friend's gesture. As she flipped through its pages, she discovered a unique feature. Certain pages had intricate illustrations and detailed instructions for specific situations, such as "When you're feeling lost," or "When you're unsure where to go." These pages caught Alberta's attention, promising guidance during uncertain times.

Filled with anticipation, Alberta embarked on her long-awaited trip to Hong Kong. The moment her plane touched down at the bustling airport, she was immediately immersed in a sea of unfamiliar sights, sounds, and scents.

Overwhelmed yet determined, Alberta clutched the guidebook tightly, relying on its wisdom.

Whenever Alberta encountered a challenging moment, she turned to the corresponding page in her guidebook. It was as if the guidebook possessed a hidden power, gently nudging her in the right direction. When she felt lost in the maze-like streets, she followed the illustrated map and found her way to stunning viewpoints overlooking the city. When she craved authentic local cuisine, she trusted the recommendations and discovered hidden food stalls serving mouthwatering delicacies.

As Alberta delved deeper into the city's vibrant tapestry, she realized that her guidebook was more than just a collection of instructions. It was a metaphorical reminder to trust her instincts, to embrace the unknown, and to have faith in herself. The guidebook taught her to navigate not only the physical realm of Hong Kong but also the intricate pathways of her own heart.

With each passing day, Alberta's journey became an adventure of self-discovery. She met kind-hearted locals who shared stories of their heritage, explored ancient temples that whispered tales of bygone eras, and wandered through bustling markets filled with vibrant colors and scents. Through it all, her guidebook remained a loyal companion, leading her towards unforgettable experiences.

Finally, the day arrived when Alberta's journey in Hong Kong drew to a close. As she stood at the airport, reflecting on the transformative adventure she had just lived, she couldn't help but feel immense gratitude for her friend, Emily, and the invaluable gift of the guidebook.

Returning home, Alberta carried the spirit of Hong Kong within her. The lessons she learned and the memories she made became a permanent part of her being. She realized that the true beauty of any journey lies not only in the destination but in the transformative power of the path itself.

And so, Alberta embarked on new adventures, armed with the knowledge that even in the face of difficulties, a little guidance and a lot of determination could lead her to the most extraordinary places in the world—both inside and outside of herself.

Discovering Hong Kong: An Overview History and Culture of Hong Kong

Hong Kong, a vibrant and dynamic city, is a unique blend of East and West. Located on the southeastern coast of China, this former British colony has evolved into a global metropolis with its own distinct identity. With a rich history and diverse culture, Hong Kong offers a fascinating journey of exploration and discovery.

Historical Background:

The history of Hong Kong can be traced back thousands of years. Its earliest known inhabitants were the indigenous people of the region, the Tanka and Hoklo communities. In the 19th century, Hong Kong became a strategic trading port during the height of the opium trade between China and Britain. The First Opium War in 1839 led to the ceding of Hong Kong Island to the British, and later, the Kowloon Peninsula and the New Territories were leased to Britain in 1860 and 1898, respectively.

Colonial Influence:

Under British rule, Hong Kong underwent rapid development and modernization. The city became an important center for trade, finance, and administration in East Asia. The British brought with them their legal, educational, and political systems, leaving a lasting imprint on the city. The rule of law, a free-market economy, and the English language became integral parts of Hong Kong's identity.

Handover to China:

In 1997, Hong Kong returned to Chinese sovereignty after 156 years of British colonial rule. This marked a significant moment in the city's history, as it became a Special Administrative Region (SAR) of China under the principle of "One Country, Two Systems." This arrangement ensured that Hong Kong retained its own legal and economic systems, as well as a high degree of autonomy, separate from mainland China.

Cultural Diversity:

Hong Kong's cultural landscape is a melting pot of influences from China, Britain, and various other countries. Chinese traditions and customs blend seamlessly with Western values, creating a unique hybrid culture. The city is home to a diverse population, including Chinese, British, and people from all over the world, contributing to its multicultural atmosphere.

Language and Cuisine:

Cantonese is the predominant language spoken in Hong Kong, but English is also widely used, reflecting its colonial heritage. The city's culinary scene is renowned worldwide, offering a vast array of options from traditional Cantonese dim sum to international cuisines. Hong Kong is a food lover's paradise, with its bustling street markets, Michelin-starred restaurants, and vibrant local food culture.

Arts and Entertainment:

Hong Kong has a thriving arts and entertainment scene. It is a hub for film, with its own influential cinema industry that has produced internationally acclaimed directors, actors, and films. The city hosts various arts festivals, exhibitions, and performances throughout the year, showcasing both local and international talents. From traditional Chinese opera to contemporary art galleries, there is something for everyone in Hong Kong's cultural landscape.

Contemporary Challenges:

In recent years, Hong Kong has faced unique challenges related to its political landscape and relationship with mainland China. The city has witnessed social and political movements advocating for greater democracy and autonomy. These events have sparked debates about identity, freedom of expression, and the future of Hong Kong.

Hong Kong's history and culture are a testament to its resilience and adaptability. It is a city that has embraced change while preserving its unique heritage. From its colonial past to its contemporary challenges, Hong Kong continues to captivate visitors with its captivating blend of Eastern and Western influences. Exploring its history, immersing in its culture, and witnessing its vibrant present is a journey that reveals the essence of this extraordinary city.

Geographical Overview and Understanding Hong Kong's Neighborhoods

Hong Kong, a vibrant and bustling metropolis located on the southeastern coast of China, is known for its unique blend of Eastern and Western cultures. The city is divided into various neighborhoods, each with its own distinct characteristics and charm. Understanding Hong Kong's neighborhoods is essential for residents and visitors alike to navigate the city and appreciate its diverse offerings.

Geographically, Hong Kong is comprised of Hong Kong Island, the Kowloon Peninsula, the New Territories, and over 200 outlying islands. The heart of the city, Hong Kong Island, is home to the Central Business District (CBD), where towering skyscrapers dominate the iconic skyline. The neighborhoods of Central, Admiralty, and Wan Chai on the island are known for their bustling streets, high-end shopping malls, and vibrant nightlife.

Across Victoria Harbor lies the Kowloon Peninsula, connected to Hong Kong Island by several tunnels and bridges. Kowloon is known for its bustling markets, cultural attractions, and diverse culinary scene. Neighborhoods such as Tsim Sha Tsui, Mong Kok, and Yau Ma Tei are popular tourist destinations, offering a mix of shopping streets, street food stalls, and historical sites like the Wong Tai Sin Temple.

Beyond Kowloon, the New Territories provide a more suburban and natural setting. This region encompasses both densely populated areas and rural landscapes. Neighborhoods like Sha Tin and Tuen Mun offer a mix of residential complexes, shopping malls, and recreational facilities. The New Territories also house picturesque landscapes, including country parks, hiking trails, and the famous Ten Thousand Buddhas Monastery in Sha Tin.

Hong Kong's outlying islands offer a retreat from the bustling urban environment. Islands such as Lantau, Lamma, and Cheung Chau are popular weekend getaways. Lantau Island is home to the iconic Tian Tan Buddha statue, Ngong Ping Village, and Hong Kong Disneyland. Lamma Island, on the other hand, offers a laid-back lifestyle with its scenic hiking trails, seafood restaurants, and charming fishing villages.

Understanding Hong Kong's neighborhoods involves considering factors such as the local culture, demographics, and amenities. The city is renowned for its efficient public transportation system, including the MTR (Mass Transit Railway), buses, and ferries, which connect different neighborhoods seamlessly.

Each neighborhood in Hong Kong has its own unique character, influenced by historical, cultural, and economic factors. From the glitz and glamor of the Central District to the vibrant street markets of Mong Kok, there is something for everyone in this cosmopolitan city.

Hong Kong's neighborhoods offer a rich tapestry of experiences, blending tradition and modernity, East and West. Whether you're exploring the bustling streets of Central, immersing yourself in the vibrant markets of Kowloon, or seeking tranquility on the outlying islands, understanding Hong Kong's neighborhoods is key to fully appreciating the diverse and dynamic city.

Chapter 1: Exploring Hong Kong Island The Central District

Hong Kong Island's Central District is a bustling and vibrant neighborhood that serves as the financial and commercial hub of the city. It is a melting pot of modern skyscrapers, historic landmarks, luxury shopping malls, and a thriving culinary scene. Here's a glimpse into the highlights of exploring the Central District in Hong Kong.

Victoria Peak: Begin your adventure with a visit to Victoria Peak, the highest point on Hong Kong Island. Take the iconic Peak Tram to reach the summit, where you'll be rewarded with breathtaking panoramic views of the city skyline, Victoria Harbour, and the surrounding mountains. The Peak also offers nature trails, restaurants, and a shopping complex.

Central Waterfront Promenade: Enjoy a leisurely stroll along the Central Waterfront Promenade, a scenic boardwalk that stretches along the harbor. Admire the picturesque views of the harbor, watch the ferries and traditional junks pass by, and take in the fresh sea breeze. The promenade is also dotted with public art installations and makes for a great spot to relax and soak in the atmosphere.

Statue Square and Cenotaph: Pay a visit to Statue Square, a historic public square in the heart of the Central District. Here, you'll find statues of prominent figures from Hong Kong's colonial past, including Sir Thomas Jackson and Queen Victoria. Adjacent to Statue Square is the

Cenotaph, a war memorial honoring the fallen soldiers of World War I and World War II.

Lan Kwai Fong: When the sun sets, head to Lan Kwai Fong, a lively nightlife district known for its vibrant bars, clubs, and restaurants. This bustling area comes alive after dark, offering a wide range of dining and entertainment options. Whether you're looking for a quiet drink or a night of dancing, Lan Kwai Fong has something for everyone.

SoHo: Just a short walk from Lan Kwai Fong is SoHo (South of Hollywood Road), a trendy neighborhood filled with art galleries, boutiques, and chic restaurants. Explore the narrow streets lined with colorful colonial-era buildings, and indulge in a diverse range of international cuisines. SoHo is particularly famous for its culinary scene, offering a fusion of flavors from around the world.

Man Mo Temple: Immerse yourself in the cultural heritage of Hong Kong by visiting the Man Mo Temple. Built in 1847, this Taoist temple is dedicated to the gods of literature (Man) and war (Mo). Admire the intricate architecture, ornate interior, and the thick coils of incense hanging from the ceiling. The temple provides a tranquil escape from the bustling city streets.

IFC Mall and Landmark: If shopping is on your agenda, make sure to visit the International Finance Centre (IFC) Mall and the Landmark. These upscale shopping complexes offer a wide range of international luxury brands, designer boutiques, and gourmet food options. Indulge in some retail therapy or enjoy a meal at one of the many high-end restaurants in these prestigious malls.

Hong Kong Park: Need a break from the urban jungle? Take a stroll through Hong Kong Park, an oasis in the heart of the Central District. This beautifully landscaped park features lush greenery, waterfalls, and a large aviary housing various bird species. Relax by the lake, explore the pathways, or visit the nearby Flagstaff House Museum of Tea Ware.

Exploring Hong Kong Island's Central District is a captivating experience that seamlessly blends tradition with modernity. Whether you're seeking breathtaking views, cultural immersion, gourmet delights, or retail therapy, this district has it all. Prepare to be enchanted by the dynamic energy and diverse attractions that make the Central District a must-visit destination in Hong Kong.

Victoria Peak and the Peak Tram

Victoria Peak, also known as "The Peak," is one of the most iconic and popular tourist attractions in Hong Kong. Situated on the western part of Hong Kong Island, it offers breathtaking panoramic views of the city's stunning skyline, Victoria Harbour, and the surrounding landscapes. The Peak is not just a mountain; it is a symbol of Hong Kong's rich history, natural beauty, and architectural marvels.

Reaching the top of Victoria Peak is an experience in itself, thanks to the historic Peak Tram. The Peak Tram is a funicular railway system that has been operating since 1888, making it one of the oldest of its kind in the world. It is a remarkable feat of engineering, conquering the steep incline of the mountain to transport passengers to the summit.

The journey on the Peak Tram begins at the Lower Terminus, located in the heart of Central district. As the tram ascends, passengers are treated to mesmerizing views of the city's skyscrapers, verdant hillsides, and the sparkling waters of Victoria Harbour. The ride is smooth and comfortable, offering a unique perspective of Hong Kong's urban landscape.

Once at the top, visitors can explore an array of attractions and activities. The Peak Tower, a distinctive landmark with its wok-like design, houses a variety of restaurants, shops, and entertainment options. It also features the famous Sky Terrace 428, an outdoor observation deck that offers a 360-degree view of Hong

Kong's skyline. The view from this vantage point is particularly breathtaking at sunset and during the Symphony of Lights, a dazzling light and sound show that illuminates the city each night.

For nature enthusiasts, there are several walking trails around Victoria Peak that showcase the region's lush greenery and diverse wildlife. The Peak Circle Walk is a popular choice, offering a leisurely stroll around the mountain with picturesque viewpoints along the way. The Victoria Peak Garden is another peaceful oasis, providing a serene environment for relaxation amidst nature.

The Peak also offers a glimpse into Hong Kong's colonial past. The Peak Tram Historical Gallery, located within the Peak Tram Lower Terminus, provides insights into the tram's rich heritage and its role in shaping the city's development. Visitors can learn about the construction process, view historical artifacts, and delve into the fascinating stories of the Peak Tram's past.

Whether it's the awe-inspiring views, the nostalgic tram ride, or the cultural and recreational offerings, a visit to Victoria Peak and the Peak Tram is an essential part of any trip to Hong Kong. It is a destination that combines natural beauty, architectural marvels, and historical significance, leaving visitors with lasting memories of this vibrant city's remarkable skyline.

Wan Chai and Causeway Bay

Wan Chai and Causeway Bay are two vibrant neighborhoods located on the northern shore of Hong Kong Island. Known for their bustling streets, rich history, and diverse attractions, these areas offer a unique blend of traditional and modern experiences. Let's explore these neighborhoods in more detail.Wan Chai, situated between Central and Causeway Bay, has a fascinating mix of old and new. It is famous for its energetic nightlife, bustling markets, and historical landmarks. One of the most iconic sites in Wan Chai is the Blue House, a century-old tenement building that has been beautifully restored and now serves as a cultural and community center. Visitors can explore the interactive exhibitions and learn about the neighborhood's heritage.

Another must-visit spot in Wan Chai is the Hong Kong Convention and Exhibition Centre, a stunning architectural marvel that has hosted numerous international events and conferences. Adjacent to it is the picturesque Golden Bauhinia Square, where you can witness the daily flag-raising ceremony, symbolizing the handover of Hong Kong's sovereignty to China.

Wan Chai is also home to a vibrant food scene. From traditional dai pai dongs (open-air food stalls) to trendy restaurants, visitors can indulge in a wide variety of culinary delights. The neighborhood offers a mix of local favorites like dim sum, roasted meats, and seafood, as well as international cuisines from around the world.

Moving eastward from Wan Chai, you'll find Causeway Bay, a bustling shopping district known for its vibrant street markets, luxury boutiques, and sprawling malls. Times Square, a towering retail complex, is the centerpiece of Causeway Bay and a mecca for shopaholics. With its extensive range of fashion brands, electronics, and lifestyle stores, it offers a shopping experience like no other.For those seeking a break from the shopping frenzy, Causeway Bay provides several green spaces to relax and unwind. Victoria Park, the largest public park on Hong Kong Island, is a popular spot for picnics, sports activities, and outdoor concerts. The park also hosts the annual Lunar New Year Fair, attracting locals and tourists alike with its festive atmosphere and traditional stalls.

Causeway Bay is also renowned for its lively street markets, such as Jardine's Crescent and Fashion Walk. These vibrant markets offer a myriad of products, including clothing, accessories, gadgets, and street food. Exploring these bustling streets is an adventure in itself, with colorful displays, aromatic food stalls, and the constant buzz of shoppers.

Both Wan Chai and Causeway Bay are well-connected to the rest of Hong Kong via an efficient public transportation network. The MTR (Mass Transit Railway) and various bus routes provide convenient access to other districts, making it easy to explore the city.

Wan Chai and Causeway Bay are vibrant neighborhoods in Hong Kong that offer a captivating blend of tradition and modernity. Whether you're interested in history, shopping, dining, or simply immersing yourself in the energetic atmosphere, these areas have something to offer everyone.

Chapter 2: Unveiling Kowloon and Tsim Sha Tsui

Kowloon and Tsim Sha Tsui are vibrant districts located on the southern tip of the Kowloon Peninsula in Hong Kong. These areas are renowned for their rich cultural heritage, breathtaking skyline, bustling markets, and diverse culinary scene. Let's take a closer look at what makes Kowloon and Tsim Sha Tsui so captivating.

Kowloon, meaning "nine dragons" in Cantonese, is steeped in history and offers a glimpse into Hong Kong's past. It is home to a plethora of attractions, including historical landmarks, traditional markets, and modern developments. One of the most iconic landmarks in Kowloon is the Wong Tai Sin Temple, a revered religious site known for its vibrant architecture and spiritual atmosphere. Visitors can witness locals praying and seeking blessings, adding to the enchanting ambiance of the temple.

For those interested in history, the Kowloon Walled City Park is a must-visit destination. It was once a lawless and densely populated city but has now been transformed into a serene park. The park showcases beautiful gardens, ancient artifacts, and remnants of the walled city, providing a fascinating glimpse into its intriguing past.

Moving towards Tsim Sha Tsui, you'll find yourself in a bustling commercial and entertainment district. The waterfront promenade along Victoria Harbour offers stunning panoramic views of Hong Kong's iconic skyline, especially during the Symphony of Lights, a dazzling multimedia light and sound show that illuminates the city's skyscrapers.

Tsim Sha Tsui is renowned for its world-class shopping experiences. The area is dotted with luxury boutiques, high-end malls, and famous shopping streets like Nathan Road, also known as the "Golden Mile of Shopping." Here, visitors can indulge in a retail therapy session, exploring a vast array of designer brands, electronics, and traditional local shops selling everything from antiques to tailor-made suits.

Art enthusiasts will find the Hong Kong Museum of Art captivating. This cultural institution houses an extensive collection of Chinese art, including calligraphy, paintings, ceramics, and artifacts, providing insights into the region's artistic heritage.

One cannot miss the Avenue of Stars, Hong Kong's version of the Hollywood Walk of Fame. It celebrates the city's film industry and pays homage to its stars. Visitors can stroll along the promenade and encounter statues of famous actors, learn about Hong Kong's cinematic history, and enjoy the stunning views of the harbor.

Additionally, the district is a culinary paradise, offering a diverse range of dining options. From traditional Cantonese dim sum to international cuisines, Tsim Sha Tsui boasts a plethora of restaurants, cafes, and street food stalls that cater to every palate.

Overall, Kowloon and Tsim Sha Tsui provide an enticing blend of history, culture, entertainment, and gastronomy. Whether you're seeking a glimpse into Hong Kong's past, a shopping spree, or simply want to admire the city's stunning skyline, these districts offer a captivating experience that will leave a lasting impression on any visitor.

Mong Kok and Yau Ma Tei

Mong Kok and Yau Ma Tei are two vibrant and bustling neighborhoods in Hong Kong, known for their rich cultural heritage, bustling markets, and vibrant street life. Located in the Kowloon Peninsula, these districts offer a unique blend of tradition and modernity, making them popular destinations for locals and tourists alike.

Mong Kok, often referred to as the "heart of Kowloon," is famous for its lively atmosphere and diverse range of activities. The area is renowned for its shopping scene, with a plethora of markets, street stalls, and shopping centers. The Ladies' Market is a must-visit for bargain hunters, offering a wide array of clothing, accessories, and souvenirs. Sneaker Street, also known as Fa Yuen Street, is a haven for sneaker enthusiasts, showcasing a vast collection of footwear and sports gear. Mong Kok is also home to the popular Langham Place, a modern shopping mall featuring international brands, entertainment facilities, and a towering 15-story atrium.

Apart from shopping, Mong Kok boasts a vibrant food scene that caters to all tastes and budgets. Visitors can savor a wide variety of local delicacies, from street food stalls serving mouthwatering snacks like fish balls and egg waffles to traditional tea houses offering classic dim sum and Hong Kong-style milk tea. The neighborhood also houses the renowned "Trendy Zone," a cluster of trendy restaurants and cafes that attract the city's hip and young crowd.

Adjacent to Mong Kok, Yau Ma Tei is another district brimming with character and charm. Known for its rich history and cultural landmarks, Yau Ma Tei provides a glimpse into Hong Kong's past. One of the iconic attractions in the area is the Yau Ma Tei Theatre, a preserved Cantonese opera theater that showcases traditional Chinese performing arts. Visitors can enjoy live performances and immerse themselves in the beauty of Chinese culture.

The district is also home to the Temple Street Night Market, a vibrant open-air market that comes alive in the evenings. The market offers a wide range of goods, including clothing, accessories, electronics, antiques, and fortune tellers. Visitors can also sample local street food at the dai pai dongs (open-air food stalls) scattered throughout the market, indulging in delicacies like clay pot rice, seafood, and grilled skewers.

Yau Ma Tei is also known for its cultural diversity, with its mix of Chinese, Indian, and other ethnic communities. The area around Shanghai Street and Kansu Street is particularly famous for its traditional herbal medicine shops, where visitors can find a plethora of herbs, dried seafood, and medicinal remedies.

In addition to its cultural and culinary offerings, both Mong Kok and Yau Ma Tei provide convenient access to various transportation options, making it easy for visitors to explore other parts of Hong Kong. The MTR (Mass Transit Railway) stations in these districts connect them to the rest of the city, ensuring seamless travel experiences.

Mong Kok and Yau Ma Tei truly epitomize the essence of Hong Kong, with their lively streets, vibrant markets, and cultural heritage. Whether you're a shopping enthusiast, a food lover, or a culture seeker, these districts offer a captivating experience that will leave you enchanted with the energy and vibrancy of this dynamic city.

The Vibrant Streets of Sham Shui Po

Nestled in the bustling metropolis of Hong Kong, Sham Shui Po is a district that boasts a unique charm and a vibrant street life. Known for its rich cultural heritage and diverse community, the streets of Sham Shui Po offer an authentic glimpse into the local way of life.

One of the defining features of Sham Shui Po is its bustling street markets. As you wander through the narrow lanes, you'll be greeted by an array of stalls selling everything from fresh produce and traditional snacks to electronics and textiles. The aroma of street food wafts through the air, enticing visitors with the tantalizing scent of local delicacies. The markets are a melting pot of sights, sounds, and flavors, providing an immersive experience for anyone eager to explore Hong Kong's street culture.

In addition to the markets, Sham Shui Po is also renowned for its thriving fabric and electronics industries. The district is home to a plethora of fabric shops and wholesale outlets, where fashion designers and DIY enthusiasts flock to find a wide variety of materials, trims, and accessories. As you stroll down the streets, you'll witness bolts of colorful fabrics adorning shopfronts, showcasing the district's rich textile heritage.

The vibrant streets of Sham Shui Po are not just about commerce; they also offer a glimpse into the district's historical and cultural significance. Within the bustling neighborhood, you'll find traditional temples and historic buildings that serve as a reminder of the area's past. One such example is the Sam Tai Tsz Temple, an 18th-century temple dedicated to the deity Sam Tai Tsz, believed to bring good fortune and protect the community. Its intricate architectural details and serene atmosphere provide a stark contrast to the hustle and bustle of the surrounding streets.

Another aspect that makes Sham Shui Po's streets come alive is the thriving local arts scene. The district has become a hub for creatives and artists, with galleries, studios, and graffiti-lined walls adorning the streets. From thought-provoking murals to avant-garde exhibitions, the art scene in Sham Shui Po adds a vibrant and dynamic touch to the streetscape, making it a visual feast for art enthusiasts and photographers alike.

Beyond the tangible aspects, it is the people of Sham Shui Po who truly bring the streets to life. Locals go about their daily routines, creating a sense of community that is unique to this district. You'll see elderly residents engaging in lively conversations, shopkeepers passionately discussing their wares, and children playing in the neighborhood parks. The diverse mix of residents, ranging from long-time residents to newly arrived immigrants, contributes to the vibrant tapestry of Sham Shui Po's streets, showcasing the multicultural fabric of Hong Kong.

The vibrant streets of Sham Shui Po, Hong Kong, offer an immersive and captivating experience for visitors. From the bustling street markets and thriving industries to the historical landmarks and flourishing art scene, there is something to enchant everyone who ventures into this district. It is a place where tradition meets modernity, where the past intertwines with the present, creating a tapestry of sights, sounds, and flavors that encapsulate the true essence of Hong Kong.

Chapter 3: Lantau Island and the Outlying Islands Discovering Lantau Island

Lantau Island is the largest island in Hong Kong and is located at the mouth of the Pearl River. Known for its stunning natural beauty and cultural attractions, Lantau Island offers a diverse range of experiences for visitors. Additionally, the Outlying Islands, which include smaller islands surrounding Lantau, provide unique opportunities to explore the lesser-known parts of Hong Kong.

One of the most iconic attractions on Lantau Island is the Tian Tan Buddha, also known as the Big Buddha. This majestic bronze statue sits atop Ngong Ping plateau and stands at an impressive height of 34 meters (112 feet). Visitors can reach the statue by taking the Ngong Ping 360 cable car, which offers breathtaking views of the island's lush mountains and the South China Sea.

Adjacent to the Big Buddha is the Po Lin Monastery, a significant Buddhist temple that attracts pilgrims and tourists alike. The monastery's serene atmosphere and beautiful architecture make it a must-visit destination for those seeking tranquility and spiritual enlightenment.

Lantau Island is also home to Hong Kong Disneyland, a world-class theme park that promises endless fun and entertainment for the whole family. With thrilling rides, captivating shows, and beloved Disney characters, the park offers a magical experience that transports visitors into the enchanting world of Disney.

For nature enthusiasts, Lantau Island boasts several picturesque hiking trails, such as the Lantau Trail and the Sunset Peak Trail. These trails wind through lush forests, mountainous terrain, and offer stunning panoramic views of the island's coastline. The island's pristine beaches, such as Cheung Sha Beach and Pui O Beach, are perfect for relaxing and soaking up the sun.

Beyond Lantau Island, the Outlying Islands provide a tranquil escape from the bustling city. Islands like Cheung Chau and Peng Chau offer a glimpse into traditional Hong Kong village life. With their narrow streets, quaint shops, and seafood restaurants, these islands exude a laid-back charm that is a welcome respite from the urban hustle.

Another notable Outlying Island is Lamma Island, famous for its vibrant arts and cultural scene. The island is dotted with art galleries, craft shops, and unique eateries, offering a perfect blend of creativity and culinary delights. Lamma Island is also known for its annual Lamma International Dragon Boat Festival, where visitors can witness thrilling dragon boat races.

To explore the Outlying Islands, ferries are available from the Central Pier in Hong Kong. The ferry ride itself is an experience, allowing travelers to enjoy the breathtaking views of the Hong Kong skyline and the surrounding waters.

Lantau Island and the Outlying Islands of Hong Kong offer a diverse range of experiences for visitors. From the majestic Tian Tan Buddha and Po Lin Monastery to the enchanting Hong Kong Disneyland and the serene hiking trails, Lantau Island is a treasure trove of natural beauty and cultural attractions. Meanwhile, the Outlying Islands provide a peaceful retreat where visitors can immerse themselves in traditional village life and vibrant arts scenes. Whether you're seeking adventure, tranquility, or a touch of local culture, Lantau Island and the Outlying Islands are sure to leave a lasting impression.

Exploring Cheung Chau

Cheung Chau, a small island located just off the coast of Hong Kong, is a hidden gem that offers a unique and delightful experience for visitors. Known for its tranquil atmosphere, rich cultural heritage, and picturesque scenery, Cheung Chau is a popular destination for both locals and tourists seeking a break from the bustling city life.

To reach Cheung Chau, you can take a ferry from Central or other designated piers in Hong Kong. As you approach the island, you'll be greeted by the sight of colorful fishing boats bobbing in the water, a charming harbinger of what's to come.

One of the highlights of Cheung Chau is its idyllic beaches. Tung Wan and Kwun Yam beaches are perfect for sunbathing, swimming, or simply enjoying a leisurely stroll along the shore. The clear waters and soft sands provide an inviting escape from the urban hustle and bustle. Water sports enthusiasts can also try their hand at kayaking, paddleboarding, or windsurfing.

Aside from its natural beauty, Cheung Chau is also steeped in history and culture. Take a walk through the narrow streets and alleyways to discover traditional Chinese architecture, quaint temples, and ancestral halls. Pak Tai Temple, dedicated to the Taoist god of the sea, is a must-visit with its ornate decorations and intricate woodcarvings. Cheung Po Tsai Cave, named after a famous pirate who once roamed these waters, offers a glimpse into the island's pirate-infused past.

Food lovers will be delighted by the culinary offerings on Cheung Chau. Fresh seafood is the highlight here, and you can savor a wide variety of dishes, from steamed fish to grilled squid, at the many seafood restaurants along the waterfront. Be sure to try the island's specialty, "dai pai dong" style cuisine, which features delicious stir-fried dishes cooked on open flames.

For a unique shopping experience, visit the Cheung Chau Market. This bustling street market is the perfect place to browse for souvenirs, local snacks, and traditional handicrafts. Don't miss the opportunity to sample the island's famous "Ma Chi" cake, a sweet pastry filled with peanuts, coconut, and sesame.

If you're up for some outdoor adventure, explore the scenic hiking trails that crisscross the island. The Mini Great Wall, a short but challenging hike, rewards hikers with panoramic views of the island and its surrounding waters. Another popular trail leads to the Cheung Chau Windmill, a restored 19th-century windmill that stands as a symbol of the island's heritage.

Whether you're seeking relaxation, cultural immersion, or outdoor exploration, Cheung Chau offers a little something for everyone. Its quaint charm, natural beauty, and rich history make it a perfect day trip or weekend getaway from the vibrant city of Hong Kong. So, set aside some time to explore this enchanting island

and create unforgettable memories in the heart of the South China Sea.

Tranquility in Lamma Island

Lamma Island, nestled just off the coast of Hong Kong, is a hidden gem that offers a refreshing escape from the bustling city life. Known for its pristine beaches, lush greenery, and laid-back atmosphere, Lamma Island exudes a sense of tranquility that is hard to find elsewhere in Hong Kong.

One of the main reasons Lamma Island is revered for its tranquility is its limited vehicle access. With no private cars or taxis on the island, the streets are free from the constant noise and pollution typically associated with urban areas. Instead, visitors and residents alike traverse the island on foot or by bicycle, creating a peaceful and unhurried ambiance.

Upon arriving on Lamma Island, it's easy to be captivated by its natural beauty. The island is home to scenic hiking trails that wind through verdant hills and offer breathtaking vistas of the surrounding sea. Whether you choose to embark on the popular Family Trail or explore the more challenging Sok Kwu Wan to Yung Shue Wan hike, you'll find yourself immersed in the tranquil embrace of nature.

Lamma Island is also known for its picturesque beaches. Lo So Shing Beach, Hung Shing Yeh Beach, and Power Station Beach are just a few examples of the island's sandy shores where visitors can unwind and soak up the sun. These beaches are rarely crowded, allowing you to enjoy a peaceful day by the sea, listening to the soothing sound of waves gently crashing against the shore.

In addition to its natural allure, Lamma Island boasts a vibrant and diverse community. The island is home to a mix of locals and expatriates, creating a unique cultural fusion. As you explore the island's quaint villages, such as Yung Shue Wan and Sok Kwu Wan, you'll find charming cafes, seafood restaurants, and boutique shops. The laid-back lifestyle and friendly atmosphere foster a sense of community, making Lamma Island an inviting place to connect with like-minded individuals or simply enjoy some solitude.

To truly embrace the tranquility of Lamma Island, it's recommended to spend the night and experience the island after the day-trippers have departed. As the sun sets, the island takes on a magical ambiance, with the sound of lapping waves and the distant glow of Hong Kong's skyline serving as a reminder of the city's proximity.

Whether you're seeking solace in nature, a peaceful beach getaway, or a break from the fast-paced city life, Lamma Island offers a serene haven that is unmatched in Hong Kong. Its unique blend of untouched landscapes, car-free streets, and a welcoming community create an atmosphere of tranquility that will leave you rejuvenated and yearning for more. So, venture off the beaten path and discover the serenity of Lamma Island for an unforgettable escape.

Chapter 4: Exploring New Territories Visiting Sai Kung and Its Surroundings

Nestled in the eastern part of Hong Kong, the Sai Kung region offers a captivating blend of natural beauty and cultural heritage. Known as the "back garden of Hong Kong," this area is a haven for nature enthusiasts and adventure seekers. From stunning landscapes to delicious seafood, Sai Kung and its surroundings provide a unique and unforgettable experience for travelers.

One of the main draws of Sai Kung is its picturesque coastline. With its pristine beaches, clear turquoise waters, and dramatic rock formations, it's a paradise for beach lovers. Sai

Kung's beaches offer a range of activities such as swimming, snorkeling, kayaking, and even stand-up paddleboarding. Some popular spots include Clear Water Bay Beach, Trio Beach, and Long Ke Wan Beach, where you can relax, soak up the sun, and enjoy the tranquil atmosphere.

For those seeking more adventure, Sai Kung is also home to the Hong Kong Global Geopark, a UNESCO-designated site. The geopark covers an expansive area and showcases a diverse range of geological formations, including volcanic rocks, sea caves, and sedimentary cliffs. Exploring the geopark's hiking trails is a fantastic way to discover its natural wonders, including the awe-inspiring hexagonal volcanic columns at High Island and the breathtaking views from Sharp Peak, the highest peak in Sai Kung.

Aside from its natural beauty, Sai Kung is renowned for its seafood. The region is dotted with fishing villages where you can savor freshly caught seafood delicacies. Sai Kung Town, in particular, is famous for its waterfront seafood market, where you can handpick your preferred seafood from the stalls and have it cooked to perfection at the nearby restaurants. From succulent prawns and crabs to mouthwatering steamed fish, the culinary experience in Sai Kung is an absolute delight for seafood enthusiasts.

To enhance your exploration of Sai Kung, consider taking a boat trip to the outlying islands. The Sai Kung Peninsula is surrounded by a cluster of islands, such as the scenic Sharp Island and the historic Kau Sai Chau. These islands offer a different perspective of the area, with their secluded beaches, lush greenery, and intriguing cultural sites. You can take a leisurely stroll along the island's trails, explore ancient temples, or simply enjoy the serenity of these hidden gems.

For history buffs, Sai Kung also boasts a rich cultural heritage. The Sai Kung Town itself has preserved its traditional charm, with its narrow streets lined with old Chinese shophouses and temples. A visit to the Tin Hau Temple, dedicated to the goddess of the sea, is a must-see, as it reflects the town's deep-rooted ties to its maritime past.

exploring Sai Kung and its surroundings in Hong Kong is an adventure that combines breathtaking natural landscapes, delectable seafood, and cultural heritage. Whether you're seeking relaxation on the beaches, embarking on outdoor activities, or immersing yourself in the local traditions, Sai Kung offers an escape from the bustling city life and invites you to discover the hidden treasures of this enchanting region.

Cultural Heritage in Tai Po

Tai Po, located in the northeastern part of Hong Kong's New Territories, is a district rich in cultural heritage. The area is known for its historical significance, traditional architecture, and vibrant local culture. From ancient temples to historic villages, Tai Po offers a glimpse into the region's past and preserves its cultural identity.

One of the prominent cultural attractions in Tai Po is the Tai Po Old Market. Dating back to the 19th century, this bustling market provides visitors with a unique experience of traditional Hong Kong street life. Strolling through its narrow alleyways, one can find an array of stalls selling fresh produce, traditional snacks, and handmade crafts. The market not only serves as a commercial hub but also as a gathering place for locals, showcasing the community's strong sense of unity and heritage.

Another notable cultural heritage site in Tai Po is the Tai Po Waterfront Park. Built on the site of the former Tai Po Hoi Shipyard, this park pays tribute to the district's maritime history. Visitors can explore the shipyard's preserved relics and enjoy the panoramic views of Tolo Harbour. The park also features recreational facilities, including cycling tracks, jogging paths, and a children's playground, providing a perfect blend of history and leisure for residents and tourists alike.

Tai Po is also home to several ancient temples that reflect the district's religious traditions and cultural practices. One such temple is the Man

Mo Temple, dedicated to the worship of the God of Literature (Man) and the God of War (Mo). Built in the 19th century, the temple showcases intricate architectural details and ornate woodcarvings. It remains a place of reverence and attracts worshippers who seek blessings for academic success or martial prowess.

Additionally, Tai Po is renowned for its historic villages, which offer a glimpse into traditional rural life. One of the most well-preserved villages is Tai Mei Tuk, located near the Plover Cove Reservoir. With its traditional stilt houses and serene waterfront setting, Tai Mei Tuk provides an idyllic escape from the bustling city life. Visitors can enjoy cycling along the scenic trails, indulge in local delicacies, and immerse themselves in the rustic charm of the village.

Preservation efforts play a crucial role in safeguarding Tai Po's cultural heritage. The Tai Po Heritage Trail, a designated route that covers various historical sites, allows visitors to explore the district's rich heritage. Along the trail, one can discover ancient walled villages, ancestral halls, and other cultural landmarks. These initiatives not only protect the architectural heritage but also promote a deeper understanding and appreciation of Tai Po's cultural roots.

Tai Po in Hong Kong stands as a testament to the region's cultural heritage. Through its ancient temples, historic villages, and vibrant marketplaces, the district showcases the richness and diversity of Hong Kong's past. By preserving and celebrating its cultural heritage, Tai Po ensures that future generations can connect with their roots and embrace the district's unique identity.

Exploring the Nature Parks of the New Territories

Hong Kong, known for its bustling cityscape and vibrant urban life, is also home to several beautiful nature parks in the New Territories. These parks offer a welcome respite from the fast-paced city life, allowing visitors to immerse themselves in the region's natural beauty, diverse wildlife, and tranquil surroundings. Here, we'll take a closer look at some of the top nature parks in the New Territories that are worth exploring.

Hong Kong Wetland Park: Located in Tin Shui Wai, the Hong Kong Wetland Park is a haven for nature enthusiasts. It spans over 60 hectares of wetland habitat, featuring a network of boardwalks and observation hides that allow visitors to explore the marshes, ponds, and reed beds. The park is home to a wide variety of plants, birds, insects, and other wetland creatures. Visitors can enjoy educational exhibitions, guided tours, and even participate in hands-on activities like bird-watching and wetland gardening.

Tai Mo Shan Country Park: As the highest peak in Hong Kong, Tai Mo Shan offers breathtaking vistas and a chance to experience the region's diverse flora and fauna. The country park covers a vast area, encompassing woodland trails, mountain streams, and scenic viewpoints. Hiking enthusiasts can embark on various trails that lead to the summit, where they can enjoy panoramic views of the surrounding landscape. The park is also known for its beautiful waterfalls, including the popular Ng Tung Chai Waterfalls.

Sai Kung East Country Park: Sai Kung East Country Park is a nature lover's paradise, boasting pristine beaches, rocky shorelines, and lush green hills. This park is particularly renowned for its hiking trails, which offer stunning coastal views and lead to hidden gems such as the picturesque Long Ke Wan Beach and High Island Reservoir. Sai Kung Town, located nearby, is a great place to refuel and sample fresh seafood at one of the many waterfront restaurants.

Kam Shan Country Park (Monkey Hill): Nestled in the hills of Kowloon, Kam Shan Country Park, also known as Monkey Hill, is a favorite among locals and visitors alike. The park is home to a large population of macaques, which are often spotted along the trails or near the park's barbecue areas. While the monkeys steal the spotlight, the park also features lush forests, serene reservoirs, and picnic spots. It's an ideal destination for a leisurely walk or a family outing.

Lantau South Country Park: Lantau Island is known for its iconic attractions like the Big Buddha and Hong Kong Disneyland, but it also offers a wealth of natural beauty within Lantau South Country Park. This park showcases the island's diverse landscapes, including rugged mountains, cascading waterfalls, and dense forests. Visitors can explore scenic trails like the Lantau Trail and the Sunset Peak, which provide breathtaking views of the surrounding islands and ocean.

When visiting these nature parks in the New Territories, it's important to respect the environment and follow park regulations. Many parks offer visitor centers with informative displays and maps, and some even provide guided tours and educational programs. So, whether you're seeking outdoor adventures, wildlife encounters, or simply a peaceful retreat, the nature parks of the New Territories in Hong Kong are waiting to be explored.

Chapter 5: Off the Beaten Path: Hidden Gems in Hong Kong and Kowloon Walled City Park

Hong Kong is a vibrant and bustling city known for its iconic skyline, bustling markets, and world-class shopping. However, beyond the popular tourist attractions lies a wealth of hidden gems waiting to be discovered. If you're looking to explore off the beaten path, here are some unique and lesser-known places to visit in Hong Kong.

Shek O Village: Tucked away on the southeastern part of Hong Kong Island, Shek O Village offers a tranquil escape from the city's hectic pace. This picturesque coastal village is famous for its beautiful beach, scenic hiking trails, and laid-back atmosphere. Enjoy a leisurely stroll along the promenade, indulge in fresh seafood at local restaurants, or simply relax on the sandy shores.

Ping Shan Heritage Trail: Step back in time with a visit to the Ping Shan Heritage Trail in the New Territories. This historical trail takes you through a series of well-preserved ancestral halls, temples, and traditional Chinese architecture. Learn about the region's rich cultural heritage and gain insight into the customs and traditions of the local villagers.

Tai O Fishing Village: Located on Lantau Island, Tai O Fishing Village provides a glimpse into Hong Kong's traditional way of life. Explore the stilt houses, narrow alleys, and bustling seafood markets that make up this charming fishing community. Take a boat ride through the village's intricate network of canals, spot the famous pink dolphins in the surrounding waters, and sample local delicacies like dried seafood and shrimp paste.

Lamma Island: Escape the urban jungle and head to Lamma Island, a peaceful oasis just a short ferry ride away from Hong Kong Island. This car-free island is known for its scenic hiking trails, beautiful beaches, and vibrant arts scene. Explore the quaint fishing village of Sok Kwu Wan, savor fresh seafood at waterfront restaurants, or simply unwind on the sandy shores.

Kowloon Walled City Park in Hong Kong

Kowloon Walled City Park stands as a testament to the rich history and fascinating past of Hong Kong's Kowloon City district. Once a notorious and densely populated slum, the area has been transformed into a serene and picturesque park that pays homage to its past. Here's why a visit to Kowloon Walled City Park is a must for history enthusiasts and nature lovers alike.

Historical Significance: The park sits on the site of the former Kowloon Walled City, a lawless enclave that thrived as a haven for crime and illicit activities until its demolition in 1993. The park's design incorporates remnants of the city's original structures, offering visitors a chance to glimpse its unique architectural features and gain insight into its tumultuous history.

Tranquil Gardens: As you explore the park, you'll discover a beautifully landscaped oasis dotted with traditional Chinese gardens, ponds, and pavilions. The meticulously manicured flora and serene surroundings provide a peaceful respite from the bustling city outside. Take a leisurely stroll along the winding paths, enjoy a picnic on the grassy lawns, or simply find a quiet spot to relax and soak in the atmosphere.

Cultural Exhibits: Kowloon Walled City Park also features several cultural exhibits that showcase artifacts and relics from the city's past. The Yamen, a restored Qing Dynasty magistrate's office, offers a glimpse into the administrative functions of the walled city. The park's exhibition hall provides further historical context through multimedia displays and informative exhibits.

Martial Arts Demonstrations: Martial arts enthusiasts will be delighted to witness the regular martial arts performances that take place in the park. Watch skilled practitioners showcase their talents in various traditional Chinese martial arts disciplines, such as Tai Chi and Kung Fu. These demonstrations provide a fascinating glimpse into the rich martial arts heritage of Hong Kong.

A visit to Kowloon Walled City Park offers a unique blend of history, culture, and natural beauty. It serves as a reminder of Hong Kong's past while providing a serene and picturesque retreat for locals and visitors alike. So, venture off the beaten path and discover the hidden gem that is Kowloon Walled City Park.

Hong Kong's Street Art Scene

Hong Kong, known for its bustling streets, towering skyscrapers, and vibrant culture, is also home to a burgeoning street art scene that has captured the imagination of locals and visitors alike. Street art, once considered an act of rebellion and vandalism, has transformed into a respected form of artistic expression, adding color, vibrancy, and a unique voice to the city's urban landscape.

Street art in Hong Kong is a diverse tapestry, reflecting a wide range of themes, styles, and influences. From graffiti to murals, stencil art to installations, the streets of this dynamic city have become an open-air gallery that showcases the talent and creativity of local and international artists.

One of the most prominent areas for street art in Hong Kong is the Central and Sheung Wan districts. These neighborhoods are dotted with narrow alleyways and hidden corners that have become the canvas for numerous street artists. The colorful murals and graffiti that adorn the walls tell stories of social issues, cultural heritage, and personal narratives, making a powerful statement amidst the bustling cityscape.

Hong Kong's street art scene is also deeply rooted in the city's rich history and cultural identity. Local artists often incorporate elements of traditional Chinese art and calligraphy into their works, creating a fusion of old and new, tradition and innovation. This blending of styles gives the art a distinctive Hong Kong flavor, bridging the gap between the past and the present.

The street art scene in Hong Kong is not limited to established artists; it also provides a platform for emerging talents to showcase their skills and gain recognition. Graffiti jams and street art festivals are regularly organized, bringing together artists from different backgrounds to collaborate, exchange ideas, and push the boundaries of their creativity. These events foster a sense of community and encourage dialogue between artists and the public, further enriching the cultural fabric of the city.

However, it is important to note that street art in Hong Kong exists in a complex socio-political context. The city's unique history and its relationship with mainland China often find expression in the art on the streets. Protest art, in particular, has gained significant attention in recent years, reflecting the city's struggle for democracy, freedom of expression, and autonomy. These powerful visual narratives serve as a form of resistance, capturing the spirit of Hong Kong's fight for its identity.

Despite its growing popularity, street art in Hong Kong still faces challenges and debates regarding its legality and preservation. While some artworks are embraced and protected by local authorities, others are subject to removal or destruction due to concerns over property rights and public order. This tension between art and the urban environment raises important questions about the role of street art in shaping the city's identity and the need for a balance between artistic expression and civic regulations.

Hong Kong's street art scene is a vibrant and ever-evolving landscape that captivates residents and visitors alike. From its diverse styles and themes to its deep-rooted connection to local culture and its role in reflecting the city's socio-political context, street art has become an integral part of Hong Kong's urban fabric. As the scene continues to evolve, it will undoubtedly contribute to the city's artistic legacy, serving as a visual testament to the creative spirit that thrives in the bustling streets of Hong Kong.

Exploring the Fishing Villages of the Sai Kung Peninsula

Nestled on the eastern shores of Hong Kong's New Territories, the Sai Kung Peninsula is a hidden gem waiting to be discovered. Known for its picturesque fishing villages, pristine beaches, and stunning natural landscapes, this area offers a unique and immersive experience for those seeking a break from the bustling city life.

One of the main draws of the Sai Kung Peninsula is its fishing heritage. Traditional fishing villages dot the coastline, showcasing the rich maritime culture of the region. Tai O, one of the most well-known fishing villages, is famous for its stilt houses that rise above the water, giving visitors a glimpse into the traditional lifestyle of the local fishing community.

Wandering through its narrow streets, you can explore local markets selling fresh seafood, dried fish, and various handicrafts. Don't forget to sample some of the delicious seafood delicacies in the local restaurants, where you can savor the flavors of the sea.

Another must-visit fishing village in Sai Kung Peninsula is Sai Kung Town itself. This charming seaside town has a vibrant waterfront promenade lined with bustling seafood restaurants, offering a wide variety of dishes to satisfy any seafood lover. Here, you can witness the daily lives of local fishermen as they unload their catch of the day. Sai Kung Town is also the gateway to the beautiful Sai Kung Country Park, which encompasses pristine beaches, hidden coves, and lush greenery.

For nature enthusiasts, exploring the Sai Kung Peninsula is an absolute delight. Sai Kung Country Park, often referred to as the "backyard of Hong Kong," is a haven for hikers, beachgoers, and adventure seekers. With numerous well-marked trails, you can embark on a journey through diverse landscapes, from dense forests and rugged hills to tranquil beaches and cascading waterfalls. Some popular hiking routes include the High Island Reservoir East Dam and the Sai Kung GeoPark, where you can marvel at unique rock formations and ancient volcanic columns.

If you're seeking a more relaxed experience, head to the Sai Kung Islands. A boat ride away from the mainland, these pristine islands offer idyllic beaches, crystal-clear waters, and abundant marine life. You can charter a sampan boat or join a guided tour to explore the islands, go snorkeling, or simply relax on the sandy shores. For a truly memorable experience, consider camping overnight on one of the uninhabited islands, stargazing under the clear night sky and waking up to the sound of gentle waves.

In addition to its natural beauty, the Sai Kung Peninsula is also home to a thriving arts and culture scene. You can explore local art galleries, visit heritage sites, or attend traditional festivals that celebrate the region's cultural heritage. The Sai Kung Tin Hau Festival, held annually, is a vibrant event featuring colorful processions, lion dances, and traditional performances.

To explore the fishing villages of the Sai Kung Peninsula, it is recommended to allocate at least a full day or even a weekend. The best way to reach Sai Kung is by public transport, with regular buses and minivans departing from various locations in Hong Kong. Once in Sai Kung, you can easily navigate the area on foot or hire a boat to access the offshore islands.

The Sai Kung Peninsula in Hong Kong offers a captivating blend of traditional fishing villages, breathtaking natural landscapes, and a rich cultural heritage. Whether you're a nature lover, a food enthusiast, or simply seeking a tranquil escape, exploring the fishing villages of the Sai Kung Peninsula promises a memorable and immersive experience that will leave you with lasting memories.

Conclusion

In the concluding chapter of "Hong Kong Travel Guide 2023: Explore and Maximize the Hidden Gems in Hong Kong," we come to the end of a thrilling journey through the vibrant city that is Hong Kong. Throughout this book, we have embarked on an exploration of the hidden gems that make Hong Kong a truly unique and unforgettable destination for travelers.

Our adventure began with a glimpse into the rich cultural heritage of Hong Kong, delving into the fascinating history and traditions that have shaped this metropolis. From the ancient temples that stand as testaments to the city's spiritual roots to the bustling markets that showcase its vibrant energy, we uncovered a tapestry of experiences that capture the essence of Hong Kong's diverse cultural landscape.

As we ventured further, we discovered the captivating neighborhoods and districts that make up the heart and soul of Hong Kong. From the narrow alleys of Central to the bustling streets of Mong Kok, each area has its own distinct character and charm. We immersed ourselves in the vibrant street art, savored the tantalizing aromas of local cuisine, and wandered through hidden enclaves where time seemed to stand still.

The book also served as a guide to Hong Kong's natural wonders, revealing the breathtaking beauty of its landscapes. From the iconic Victoria Peak, where we witnessed a mesmerizing skyline, to the tranquil beaches and lush hiking trails, we found solace in the city's remarkable blend of urban and natural environments. These hidden treasures reminded us of the importance of preserving and cherishing the delicate balance between nature and modernity.

Moreover, the book strived to provide practical advice to help readers maximize their experience in Hong Kong. From tips on navigating the bustling transportation system to recommendations for off-the-beaten-path attractions, we aimed to empower travelers to uncover the city's hidden gems at their own pace. By encouraging exploration beyond the well-trodden tourist paths, we hoped to inspire a deeper connection with Hong Kong and foster a sense of adventure in every reader.

Ultimately, the magic of Hong Kong lies not only in its towering skyscrapers or famous landmarks but in the hidden gems that exist just beneath the surface. It is a city brimming with surprises, awaiting those willing to embark on an unforgettable journey of discovery.

As we conclude this travel guide, we hope that it has served as a source of inspiration, guiding you towards the lesser-known aspects of Hong Kong. May it encourage you to step off the beaten path, engage with the locals, and uncover the hidden stories that lie within this enchanting city. Whether you are a first-time visitor or a seasoned traveler, we invite you to immerse yourself in the vibrant tapestry of Hong Kong, to explore its hidden gems, and to create memories that will last a lifetime. So go forth, wander, and

let the secrets of Hong Kong unfold before your
eyes.

Printed in Great Britain
by Amazon

28806455R00057